I0829401

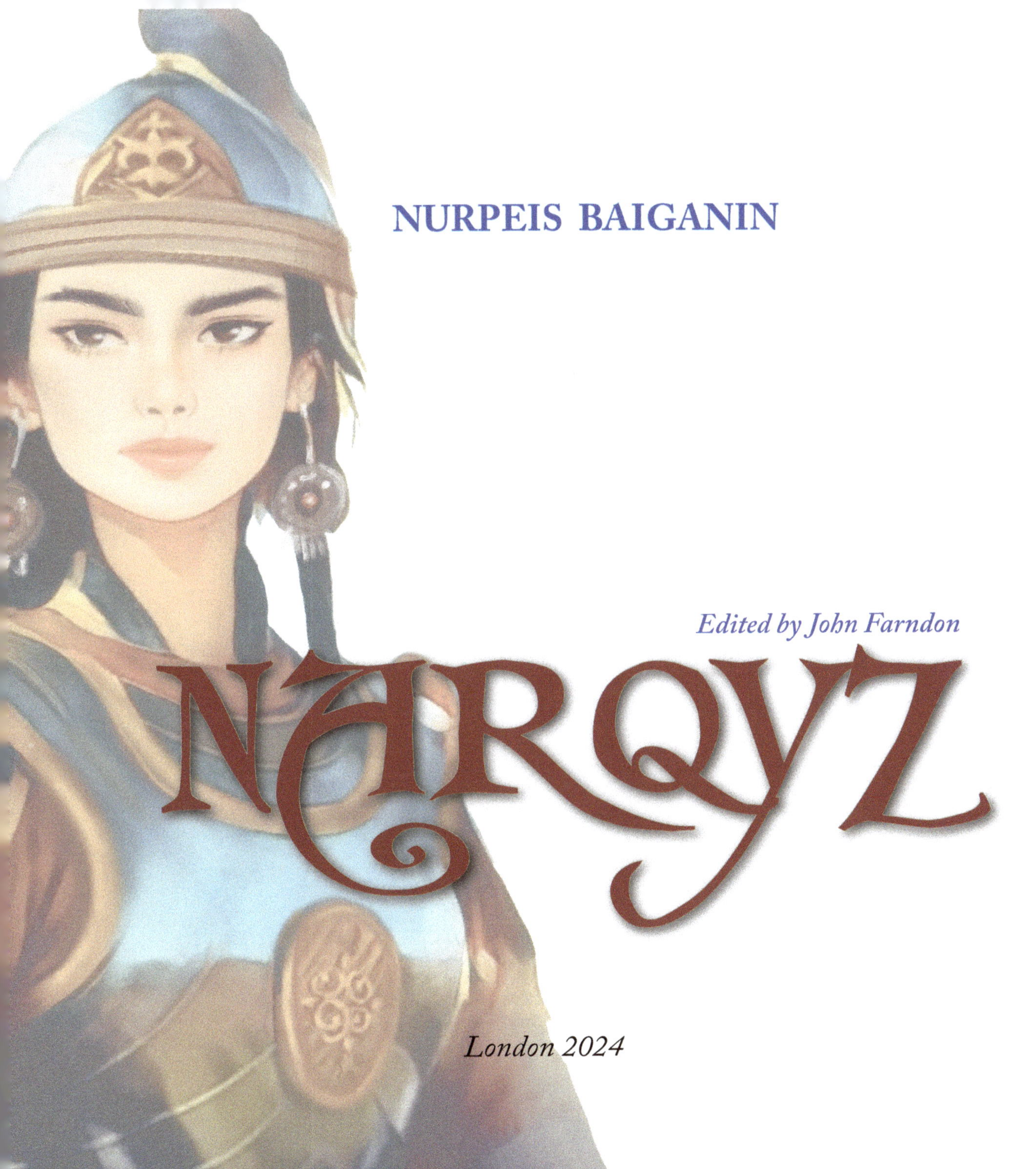

NURPEIS BAIGANIN

Edited by John Farndon

NARQYZ

London 2024

Published by Hertfordshire Press Ltd © 2024
e-mail: publisher@hertfordshirepress.com
www.hertfordshirepress.com

NARQYZ

NURPEIS BAIGANIN

*This publication presents to the reader the epic poem "**Narqyz**", by national aqyn (poet improviser) Nurpeis Baiganin.*

Edited by John Farndon
Translated by Elden Sarybay
Illustrated by Akmaral Zharaskyzy
Designed by Alexandra Rey

---

*British Library Catalogue in Publication Data
A catalogue record for this book is available from the British Library
Library of Congress in Publication Data
A catalogue record for this book has been requested*

ISBN: 978-1-913356-71-2

CONTENTS

FORCWORD

The word on the steppes

Even in Kazakhstan, this epic poem Narqyz is a precious cultural artefact, as well as a great story. So it is wonderful to see Kazakh poet and troubadour Nurpeis Baganin published in English, in a new translation. The poetic treatment of the text is based on the semantic original text of the epic. It is precious because it is an almost unique preservation of a remarkable artistic tradition of oral poetry.

For thousands of years, oral poetry was at the heart of our European culture. Spoken poetry was the way stories were passed down from generation to generation, preserving our unique heritage and reinforcing each nation's cultural identity with every telling and retelling. Of course, in the millennia before TV and pop, poets not only sustained the memories of the nation's heroes – they were heroes themselves, holding people spellbound in a shared imaginative experience that helped bind communities. They were celebrities, the best creating a thrill when they turned up to strut their stuff.

But in Europe that dynamic, oral tradition vanished long ago, along with many of the stories the poets told. Recently, of course, young rap and performance poets have excitingly revived the idea and are bringing huge new audiences to poetry. And yet they are entirely cut off from European tradition.

That's what makes this work so fascinating. A nomadic people, most Kazakhs didn't have printed books until recently, and yet they are a highly literate people, and oral poetry, storytelling, and music stayed integral to their lives for thousands of years and has survived even to the present day. It came under grave threat during the soviet era, when all forms of independent culture came under attack, but it is now undergoing something of a revival.

The torchbearers of this ancient oral tradition were the aqyns and zhiraus. Aqyns and zhiraus are something like troubadours, telling stories in rhyme, accompanying themselves with traditional instruments like the dombra or korbuz. But while zhiraus specialize in recounting the old epic stories, aqyns are masters of improvising, making up poems on the spot, in accordance with strict rules. They can base their poems around anything from ancient stories, to contemporary events. The thrill for audiences is not only in the story, but seeing how brilliantly and surprisingly they turn a phrase.

Even today master aqyns are highly revered – and highly competitive. For thousands of years, they have been bidding to outdo each other in aitys - which are poetry contests a bit like rap battles, but organized not by local clubs but by chieftains in the past, but now by TV companies, with major prizes, making them rather like a poetic X Factor.

The limitation, or maybe the glory, of the works of aqyns is that before the age of TV recordings it was ephemeral. People might know the fame of great aqyns of the past, but no-one knows any of their work, because of course it was not written down.

So this long poem rather special, because we have it here preserved. Baganin was born in 1860, while the oral tradition of Kazakh poetry was still at its height, and he grew up to become a renowned aqyn himself, gaining great acclaim at aitys events across the country. Like many great aqyns before him, Baganin didn't simply retell the old stories; he reimagined them to reflect the modern world around him. And unlike other aqyns from the millennia old pre-Soviet tradition, he wrote some of his work down, and this epic is one of them. So while we do not have the thrill 7 of his live, improvised performances, we at least in this volume get a glimpse of his extraordinary storytelling ability, building on generations of skills by previous aqyns.

Unusually, one might think, its batyr, its warrior hero, is not a man but a woman. But despite the frequently patriarchal nature of Kazakh society, women frequently play heroic roles in ancient Kazakh stories. So prepare to read about the adventures of Narqyz, and imagine the story being told through the night around a fire in a large tent on the steppes with the muffled sound of the wind outside, the steady thrum of the dombra and the rise and fall of the aqyn's voice as he recounts his tale.

John Farndon,
London, November 2023

*In loving memory
of my grandmother Aimeken,
wife of Nurpeis Baiganin*

NARQYZ

A tale of old, let me unfold,

From theLesser Horde union, Alim tribe so bold,

Of Alshyn folk in days of yore,

Listen, dear people, to your old man's lore.

Seit's daughter Aisha,

Radiant as the moon's soft gleam,

Though humble in means, she held a wondrous dream,

Her talent knew no bounds, a gift so rare,

A multitude of skills, beyond compare.

She sang melodies sweet, music her delight,

With the dombra's strings, she reached pure height,

Her voice wove fables, captivating all around,

In awe, the crowd stood, by enchantment bound.

A famed wrestler, known to all,

Against undefeated champions she'd stand tall,

Mighty opponents, numerous and near,

Couldn't get her to fall, free from fear,

Never once did she falter or quell.

In horse races she vied with grace,

Appreciation and blessings adorned her pace.

As enduring as a dromedary's stride – Nar,

And as fair as a maiden, a radiant star – Qyz,

From a young age they called her "Narqyz."

Whosoever glimpsed her visage fair,

Radiated like the moon's celestial glare,

Her demeanor graced with charm so true,

Endearing to all, hearts in admiration grew.

To questions smart she answered wise,

Her calves like cribs, a mother's guise,

Her chest as vast as a welcoming door,

Wide shoulders strong, her presence more.

Beneath her shawl a braid did flow,

Massive and proud she let it grow.

Her outer grace, surpassed that of men,

Beauty inherent, effortless, then,

No need for trying, no artifice there,

Her radiance natural, beyond compare.

In crowded places, her songs would unfurl,

Like mountain springs gushing, a musical swirl,

Arts, beauty, strength, a fusion so grand,

All traits combined, in her heart's command.

Adored by those around, her presence grand,

With dombra in hand, she'd understand,

A celebration of music and cheer,

Her wisdom shining crystal clear,

Loved by all, she'd brightly stand.

At that time, at that place

Khan Mambet rules the space.

The folk under his supervision

Were not in the best of conditions.

The khan's elder brother, bald and plain,

Not known for wits, nor wisdom's gain,

Yet content he was, in a simple way,

For the khan, his brother, held sway…

An edict of weight from Khan Mambet's command,

"Find my brother a wife,"

From Seit with force he did demand,

No choice remained, as Khan's word held tight,

No room for dissent, nor prolonged fight;

"I can't defy the khan," Seit voiced his thought,

"I stand not in power; my hands are caught."

From the envoy's lips, the news did stun,

Gasps resounded under the sun,

Narqyz fell silent, thoughts taking flight…

Then courage bloomed, a fire burning bright:

"My life is beyond measure, it's true,

I won't obey father, and no matter who,

To the bald man's whim, I won't concede,

Or marry him, I will be free.

Dombra's mastery is my claim,

For the world's horizons, I'll boldly aim.

Though they would have me restrain,

Amongst my people I shan't remain,

Equals I'll seek, who think the same!..."

The camel-eyed beauty so declared,

Upon her white-coated steed, she fared,

By the fringes, her dombra hung with grace,

To lands unknown, her steps would trace.

Her family witnesses, understanding flows,

The fire within, her anger surely shows.

Among her closest kin, compassion stirs,

"Poor young camel-eyed," their words confer,

Heartache they sense, but don't deter.

Where nomads roam, vast and free,

The Khan's dominion reached as far as the eye could see…

Royal guards flanked him, an imposing sight,

Khan Mambet adorned in regal light,

Lead the migration to the next site.

A fox fur hat upon his head did rest,

Atop a white horse, he rode his best,

A silver-hilted whip, emblem of might,

In his grasp, held power's sight,

And across khan's path some stranger strayed,

And as they crossed, no respect was paid…

Upon this sight, Khan Mambet spoke,

Annoyance in his tone bespoke,

- Since Khan I became, he said aloud,

To my authority, all heads have bowed,

I've brought happiness to khandom's domain,

Esteemed by all, my rule's refrain.

Ruling my people, meeting theirs needs

What, as a khan, have I not achieved?

Never ere this, have I did meet,

One who dared cross the path beneath my feet.

Five of my guards, who beside me stand,

Go fetch the young one who defied my command.

The lad who crossed the khan's domain,

Bring him forth, have him restrained.

Teach him the weight of respect's decree,

When the Khan approaches, let him see,

How dare he disregard honor's creed.

But listen closely, dear and keen,

A secret the poet's words convene,

The stranger passing, was no lad unknown,

The one who crossed Khan's path alone,

Is none other than we know so well,

Narqyz, the girl, in the tale's swell.

The horse she rode, she urged with whip,

Away from the guards, in flight she'd slip,

From five men's grasp, she fled with speed,

Over a hill her steed did lead.

The other side lush with grasses spread,

A haven to hide, away from men's tread,

She dismounts the horse with care,

Girth and saddle, she secures them there,

She won't flee, nor cower away,

From those five men, she'll stand, she'll stay.

With spear and sword within her grip,

She charges forth, a determined trip,

Striking with the spear, fierce and bold,

Her cotton robes, armor to hold.

Unyielding to their weapons' might,

Her layers of cotton stand the fight,

Some backed off, retreating from her view,

Those who remained, a challenge they'd pursue.

Narqyz, unyielding, made her stand,

A difficult battle for the determined band.

Narqyz ignited the skirmish's flame,

Facing all five without trembling or shame,

Anger ablaze within her heart.

She dismounted with purpose from the start,

One by one, she pulled them down,

From their saddles, her prowess renowned.

Breathless and weary, their spirits frayed,

Together as one, they yielded and prayed,

"Have it your way," adding, "brother man."

Said to Narqyz one of the soldiers then.

The valiant girl spoke, her words ablaze,

"Listen, all of you," her voice did raise,

"Sense resides in everyone's heart,

When a sheep fears a donkey's part,

They call her sister, in kindness sway,

Warriors, brothers, in their words they weigh,

Mistaken you are, in words you employ,

Do you realize that now, boys?

You pursued me, thoughtless and blind,

Without care for what's on my mind,

Had you not addressed me as 'brother' in jest,

Your eyes I'd have claimed, with anger expressed.

But in the end, you bowed to the fray,

In yielding, your stubbornness did sway,

You couldn't acknowledge me as 'elder sister,' true,

And from a 'brother,' forgiveness you drew.

You've witnessed me now, my presence revealed,

Yet my name remains a secret, concealed.

Go to your khan, let him know,

That you've met a poet soul.

Not a poet but a warrior cold…

Could he be on par, an equal to find,

When he's bested by a woman's bind?

Time's not to squander, hasten away,

Go mount your horses, I say.

On a slim steed, swift in its grace,

A racing champion, a noble chase,

Reins lost, it dashed in wild spree,

A runaway frenzy, unbridled and free.

Spotting us, it leaped in flight,

A bird-like bound, a wondrous sight.

Galloping faster, its speed never slowed,

Over holes in the ground, it nimbly rode,

Our mounts couldn't match its rapid stride,

Left in its wake, unable to coincide.

A rider's silhouette was just a figure in view,

But who it was, we couldn't know, it's true.

Unable to close in, our pursuit in vain,

Riding far and wide, efforts waned,

The figure vanished from our gaze.

What means had we against this rider fast?

Purposeful, surely, he crossed your path,

Aware of the steed's astonishing speed,

We affirm this truth, our khan, please heed!.. –

So the five men recounted, so they begun

When they reached the khan, their story spun.

Mambet lent ear to their tale's embrace,

Upon their words, he fixed his gaze,:

My guards, my advisors,

An interesting person, indeed, I must say,

Who is this omnipotent figure, I pray?

Why hasn't he come to bow to me in fealty,

And crossed my path unceremoniously?

A khan's being is his authority

So this fugitive must be sought

My order to him must be brought!

Khan Mambet's fury flared high,

At the white-horsed rider passing by,

Why provoke my ire? Exclaimed the sire,

He spat the following command like fire:

"Search for this rider, I decree,

Cursed by skies, may his fate be,

Catch him, hold tight, don't let him flee.

Disgraced by him, my heart's unease.

He who disrespected,

And my ire ignited,

Neglecting my station,

The one who slighted me, my spite I'll show.

Today he eludes,

But tomorrow he'll know!

Mambet's clarity in command stands tall,

His captains understand it all,

And immediately they comply with the call.

Simple folk and hunters in stride,

Determining where the rider might hide,

Supervised by captains by their side.

Should they spot one on a steed white,

They bring him before the khan's sight.

Answers they seek

Through interrogation's door,

Whips in hand, their methods sure.

Having tortured many, only tears they find,

The captains, sleeves rolled up, not far behind.

Scouting anew, with determination, they roam,

Seeking the answers that stay unknown.

White horses no longer grace the ride,

People abandon them by the tide.

News spread like wildfire, wide and free,

Among the people, a tale to decree.

Hearing this, Narqyz's mind did spark,

Contemplating thoughts within the dark:

"I'll approach Khan Mambet's door,

Display my courage, my heart's uproar,

Fearless, provide answers he seeks for;

Or perhaps I should hide,

Retreat completely from the light,

Ponder my steps in the cover of night;

Should a gathering emerge, where I can dare,

I'll ride my white horse and boldly declare,

Before the khan, with courage untamed,

Fearless, I'll step forward, unashamed.

Yet the khan, ruthless and dread,

Many fear him, where his influence spread.

Without a crowd, going alone's a plight,

For his friends abound, his reach is tight.

Alone I'd be a captive, without a doubt,

A pray for their clutches with no way out.

Yet in a crowd is a different scene,

I'll share my thoughts, open and keen.

A people's embrace won't let me be snared,

Safe from the khan's grasp, their shield declared.

In a public space, my voice will sound,

All my thoughts I will unbound.

Eyes will witness the power I hold,

My work and strength, a story bold.

Though alone now, fleeing Khan's domain,

Let them witness my struggle, my pain.

In a public space, my truth unveiled,

The people's support, my tale impaled.

At grand gatherings, be it feast or funeral's bell,

I'll challenge him to wrestle, my spirit to swell.

With the gathered witnessing my prowess well."

These are Narqyz's thoughts

With decisiveness in her hear,

And with her determination rising

Narqyz doesn't back down.

Yet no grand feast or gathering, near or far,

In the coming days or year's bright star.

With well-fed livestock and people in reprieve,

Survived the winter, a season to believe.

The next summer dawned, hunger in their gaze,

A feast they longed for, a communal blaze…

Last autumn, Zharlygas left this plain,

To honor the wealthy man's domain,

To honor his memory, invitations flew,

To a commemorative feast, a gathering due.

To the inviting party, respects they paid,

Invitations accepted, a gathering laid.

As the commemoration's day drew near,

The deceased's wife found solace clear.

Every tribe was present in array,

Alshyn, Zhappas, a lot of Shekti came that day,

All twelve branches of Baiuly, in unity rode

Through roads and dust, respect they showed.

The ruling lord attended, a presence known,

To the feast's orchestrator, his honor shown.

For respecting tradition and ancestral decree,

He bestowed some leaves in a pure silver jug for tea.

Offering help and service, true and sincere,

To the family gathered, a gesture clear

The Zhagalbaily and Zhetiru came to share the pain

Riding their horses from their plains.

Tama and Tabynga, they also came,

To join in prayer, to honor the name.

From distant horizons, where horses may stride,

Ramazan, Toleuge, and more by their side,

Kerderi and Kereitke, arrived from far and wide.

At this gathering grand, the tribes combined,

A feast of splendor for a memory defined.

Kumyz like rivers, in abundance flowed,

Drinking and revelry, a festive ode.

If just the guests that came on mounts

Five hundred eighty horses one could count.

Even more strongmen arrived with zest,

To compete at the feast, to put to the test.

Subduing opponents on the mat, they vied,

Horse and camel races, they aimed to ride.

Their prowess they showcased, or they tried…

Strongmen came from everywhere, it seems

Boasting of their own might and deeds

And oh-so proud of their frisky steeds.

The feast brought fame to many a name,

Livestock slaughtered for the guests to claim.

A lake of their blood formed a vivid sight,

Symbolic of unity, for the tribes' delight.

Long-separated relatives have met anew,

Exchanging greetings, spirits renew.

The commemoration brought many delights

And the event lasted seven days and nights.

Those who came to race their mounts,

Excitedly shouted, "Let's race!" in counts.

And to have a race finish line,

So those from who came from afar.

For this, the host was deemed fit to speak,

Acknowledged by all, his blessing they seek.

Dressed for the occasion, his attire bold,

On a snow-white horse, a sight to behold

Adorned in splendor, a sight to behold,

In all-black cotton, the tale's fabric unfold.

Noble and revered, his presence grand,

Respected by all, across the land.

With manners surpassing her peers around,

Wearing vibrant attire, a sight so profound.

Gilded ornaments on her trousers, bright,

Her round face appealing, a captivating light.

Hair neatly bound,

And a hat in place,

An ornate belt adorning her waist.

With an air of mystery, and no revelation,

Narqyz arrived at the commemoration.

The gathering took place

At the Embah's grand expanse,

Bushes and shrubs in this land did abide.,

With Steppe wormwood spread far and wide.

Guests gathered, climbing with fervent will,

Chaotic in their ascent to the top of a hill.

A young man sped by,

On camelback he did ride,

And on an elm tree's branch,

A flag he hung up very high,

In his hand he held it, the wind as his guide.

From midst the crowd, five riders emerged,

Dust rose in Embah's land, commotion surged.

As the hill's peak they all did reach,

A decision was made, a lesson to teach.

"Riders, listen up," the directive clear,

"No striking allowed, let this be sincere.

The kids on the hilltops will watch with intent,

Instruct them well, your actions prevent.

When riders return, bring us the news,

Stay vigilant, make sure they don't snooze.

Watch out for them, their safety's key,

Report back to us, their guardians be."

From the race's start line,

The children's joy in sight,

They dashed to their stations, hearts light.

The racing grounds' span, as tales do attest,

Two camping trips' distance, a challenging test.

Around hilltops, they swiftly convened,

Settling to watch, their interest keen.

Amidst yelling and noise, the scene's pace,

They moved along the track, a dynamic race.

In Embah's, noise filled the air,

Dust rose from the ground, a sight to share.

Watching the race, hearts raced in tune,

Beating faster, under the sun's noon.

Excitement reigned the atmosphere's swoon!...

The eyes have seen races, a spectacle's delight,

Now came time for wrestling, a test of might.

Voices around echo, a unified shout,

"Let the wrestlers come out!" their cry devout.

In a circle they sat, the people around,

Spreading out so that space could be found.

All the wrestlers emerged, ready to face,

A spectacle awaited, an eager embrace.

With bated breath, anticipation in the air,

People waited, curious and aware.

A wrestler girl stepped forth in view,

Seasoned in contests, her skills true.

Pay heed now, hold your gaze tight,

Don't miss this part, a scene of light.

Eyes gleamed like diamonds, a radiant sight,

Her stride confident, like a fortress's might.

Gaze upon her form, your passion set free,

A sight to behold, an enchanting decree!..

In a gold jacket adorned with care,

Velvet trousers, attention they ensnare.

A sash belt adorned her waist,

Her heart soared high, in spirit's embrace.

With fiery determination, she addressed the crowd,

"Come on, wrestlers!" she exclaimed aloud,

Narqyz laughed, her gaze held proud.

Never has there been, it's plain to see,

An equal to Narqyz, a truth set free.

Wrestlers' spirits faltered when she drew near,

In her presence their uncertainty appeared.

When Narqyz the wrestler stepped in the ring,

Others went for a walk, their fear taking wing.

Before Narqyz wrestled, she readied with care,

Stretched her muscles, focused in the air.

Addressing the audience, her voice clear and true,

Words to those who gathered, her intentions to construe:

A woman by birth, Narqyz is my name,

Since I was born, this title I claim.

Not one to boast, let actions portray,

Many wrestlers have tried

I've brought them down,

No one dares to challenge, none to be found.

At this joyful gathering's embrace,

I've yet to wrestle, a vacant space.

Surely a challenger will rise, I know,

The people are aware of my strength's glow.

Is there anyone here, in this festal crowd,

Who'll face me in challenge, strong and proud?

If a wrestler of my rank stands near,

Step forward, where are you, dear?

Khan Mambet's voice rang,

Commanding and loud,

Summoning wrestlers, a challenge endowed.

The first to heed the call's resounding shout,

A warrior emerged, "The Giant" with a glout.

To seize the honor, from below he came,

"The Giant" they called him, a warrior of acclaim.

His reputation echoed far and wide,

A name known for strength, a towering stride.

Horses and camels he could retrieve,

That fell into wells, a feat hard to believe.

At the name Narqyz, his interest set ablaze,

A desire to wrestle, a challenge to raise,

Hastening to the ring, clearing the ways.

His strength and valor, none could deny,

A wrestler of note, standing high,

His build and weight like a mountain nigh,

His visage broad, a face of strength,

A wrestler unmatched, of considerable length.

The crowd stood up in anticipation.

In a kaftan he stood, broad trousers on,

Eyes ablaze, a challenge to dawn.

To wrestle Narqyz, his determination clear,

A fiery match, drawing near.

Facing off, they locked in a grip,

Wrestling fiercely, their strengths to equip,

Neither could dominate, neither could skip.

Unyielding, neither surrendered their might,

Tripping each other proved a daunting task,

Struggling on, both with equal fight.

A mighty soul indeed, resolute and strong,

Refusing to be brought down, wrestling long.

Proud to a fault, unwilling to yield,

Fighting to remain upright on the field.

An uncle of Narqyz

Then came to the fore,

Noticing her torn collar,

Concern he bore.

To aid Narqyz, with care he spoke,

Listen now, his words I quote:

- You're Narqyz, the wrestler, he proclaimed,

I'm Kenzhe, your uncle, he exclaimed.

Did the Most High forsake you, my kin?

Has your strength left you, giving in?

What's taking so long?! - He urged her to win.

They want what you want,

All of these people here, he said.

Take down the khan's wrestler, he implored,

Strip him of his pride, let your strength be poured.

"Argh!" Narqyz cried with all her might,

A fearless woman ending the fight,

She spun him around, with strength so profound,

Feet firm on the ground, her power unbound.

Like a tumbleweed, he lay in defeat,

The khan's warrior conquered, his strength deplete.

Spitting bloody foam, his mouth painted bare.

Water splashed upon his face with care,

Through effort, he awoke from his wrestling affair…

The khan's face paled, offense taking root,

Mambet shamed, his pride set to mute.

"One more of you," he commanded anew,

His wrestlers prepared, a challenge to pursue.

Another of the khan's wrestlers appeared in sight,

A hefty, dark man, known for his might.

Strong as well, his reputation stood,

Should the khan's wrestler meet his demise,

He'd be no better than the common folk guys.

Gazing upon his face, camel-like and tough,

Stout and sturdy, appearing gruff.

He drew near, casting glances aside,

Focused on Narqyz, his challenge to ride.

With a firm grip, he clasped her strong,

Ready to wrestle, prove his brawn.

But his wrestler hesitated, mercy took hold,

A compassionate heart, his demeanor bold.

Holding Narqyz in his grasp so tight,

The khan's warrior spoke, his voice taking flight:

"You are named Narqyz, he declared to the skies,

And I've come to wrestle, he said with no lies.

A woman's path is more important than men's,

This match, Narqyz, I make it thine.

Choose your path, let your victory shine."

Narqyz spoke to the wrestler with grace,

Observing his age in her words' embrace.

"Though I'm a girl and you are older," said she,

"You'll take your own path, brother, let it be.

Eyes surround us, watching this bout,

Let them witness, without a doubt,

Who's the wrestler, who's the weak,

Let the people judge, let their voice speak!"

Released by Narqyz, the wrestler did shake,

Gazing at her, not knowing what to make.

Narqyz stood firm, her feet held their ground,

Waiting for a challenge, strength unbound.

The wrestler noticed her determination clear,

Ready to endure more, showing no fear.

From her spot, Narqyz stood her ground,

None of his moves could make her rebound.

He aimed to trip her, to force a sway,

But Narqyz remained steadfast in the fray,

None of his attempts led her astray.

Striving to appear stronger, he tried in vain,

But Narqyz's strength remained a steadfast chain.

Seeing her resolve, he yielded, saw the light,

Narqyz's power too great to fight.

The wrestler girl's prowess shone bright,

A spectacle witnessed by all in sight.

The people's voices roared her name,

A lion's roar, igniting the flame.

Witnessing this, the common folk sighed,

"Narqyz is truly wondrous," they cried.

Her steadfast stance, her power displayed,

Throwing the khan's warriors as if a charade.

They marveled at her strength, her might,

Defeating them with sheer delight.

Observing the people's affection with a frown,

Mambet's mood descends, a troubled crown.

As ruler, his patience wears thin,

His trusted wrestlers, they couldn't win.

How could he not feel vexed and sore,

As both his champions hit the floor?

- May your strength be boiled!" Mambet declared,

This challenge is tough, my anger's flared.

Begim, my strongman, where do you hide?

Known as "The Lion," let your power be your guide.

My fury's ablaze, sweat on my brow,

Time to act boldly, show us how.

Tear from the belly of the beast,

The khan's pride, his throne's might,

From this commoner, rip it wide!

"The Lion" wrestler, fierce and famed,

Against many a foe, he's been acclaimed.

His visage seemed weary, burdened and gray,

Pride and pressure taking their toll, they say.

From afar he came to the fore,

To wrestle Narqyz, a challenge to explore.

He shed his robe,

Donned a jacket instead,

Dirty white in color, worn from his tread.

His visage matched his rugged demeanor,

A face that told tales, weathered and cleaner.

His legs resembled those of a sturdy camel,

Strong and resilient, like an ancient anvil.

Chest as wide as gates, strength in his name,

Built like a tree trunk, known by his frame.

One thing stood out, his thickness, no doubt,

A hulking presence, his reputation stout.

He made his way to the wrestler Narqyz

Who was sitting down.

And when he got close

The unflinching brave Narqyz

Grabbed him by his hips.

The onlookers within the crowd,

Yelled and cheered, their voices loud.

The wrestlers clashed in a bout,

Grappling fiercely, no doubt.

Striving to outmaneuver and best,

Each other's strength put to the test.

Both striving with might and skill,

In this wrestling match, a test of will.

Then Mambet's voice rose, a powerful sound:

- Hey little brother, the Lion so bold,

In this wrestling match, let your zeal unfold.

Is it not shameful, the time you take,

To defeat a girl, for goodness' sake?

You're tarnishing my name with each delay,

Wrestling Narqyz, what do you say?

Taking so long, oh, what a disgrace,

A woman's might outshines your base.

You're a man, and yet a woman prevails,

How is it that your honor trails?

You'd rather die than face such plight,

Then walk this earth after losing this fight!

The Lion was stung by words so severe,

He gathered strength, fueled by his fear.

No respite for Narqyz, he pressed on,

Employing every tactic he had drawn.

Narqyz was upset,

Her face turned pale,

Her collar torn,

Her spirit frail.

Amidst the crowd,

Her uncle Kenzhe came,

Brother of Seit,

And voiced his claim.

"My dear Narqyz, my soul's delight,

Why is your breath labored, in this fight?

In this crucial hour, we're by your side,

Have you lost your strength, your stride?

Sister Narqyz, don't give up the race,

Your people stand with you, embrace the grace!.."

In that instant, Narqyz felt a surge

Of power coursing through like a river's verge.

Honor and anger intertwined within,

Her spirit ignited, ready to win.

All gathered there, wide-eyed they stared,

At Narqyz's strength that flared.

She pushed, she lifted, with power untamed,

The wrestler who struggled, his pride now maimed.

Turning to Khan Mambet, she spoke with pride:

- Listen closely, Mambet, she declared,

I'm Narqyz, and I'm unimpaired.

Your widowed brother, do you believe

He's my equal? I'll make you perceive.

Your little brother, this little Lion cub

Watch what I do with him, she said with a snub.

Let everybody see him now!

No room for disgrace, I vow.

You made life tough, played your part,

But I'm Narqyz, with strength at heart.

Why should I bear cowardice's plight?

Witness Narqyz's power, with all your might.

Your little brother, The Lion here,

I'll defeat before you, so crystal clear.

She strikes him down to the floor,

Drops him with a force to abhor,

And from the force of the beating

The wrestler's nose starts bleeding.

Broken and shaken, he returns,

Before Khan Mambet, his spirit yearns,

He beats the ground, his pride denied,

His backbone of his pride,

Fractured inside.

Like a chopped wooden stump,

He's brought low, a defeated lump.

Then Mambet cries, his voice forlorn,

My happiness, have you truly gone?

Are you upset with me?

Not by a man, but a woman's hand,

My own blood brother lies defeated,

My dreams shattered in the sand.

The Lion wrestler, once fierce and bold,

Now lay defeated, his consciousness cold.

Nobles surrounded him, seeking aid anew,

From the commoners, helpers they drew.

Lifting him gently, they moved him aside,

Carrying him away, his strength denied.

Narqyz showcased her might with grace,

Bringing tears to the rulers,

And a smile to every other face.

"Be a wrestler like Narqyz," they now say,

"Even the Lion of the clan couldn't hold his sway,

With broken bones, he's been led away."

The crowd erupted in cheer,

They were full of glee,

As Khan's mighty warrior fell,

For all the world to see.

Then a message from Mambet

To Narqyz was relayed.

The messenger boy conveyed:

Let Narqyz come to me, - Mambet's words to bear,

If she bears a grudge against my name,

Let her come and explain, no need for blame. – He said.

Narqyz should realize,

That I am the khan – He said.

Not to mingle among common folk's cheer,

To me directly, she should come near. – He said.

If Narqyz is wise, he stated with might,

She'll comprehend my rank, do what is right.

Since the Lion's defeat,

My mood's turned dark,

Let Narqyz come to me, make her embark."

Such was his invitation he sent.

If a khan tells one to come

Who of the people wouldn't obey?

But Narqyz looked at the matter

And thought about not going.

The people held their heads

And kept telling her:

"it isn't so difficult

The khan is the protector the realm.

Going against his wish would be wrong."

So the elders urged her to go.

With courage undeterred, Narqyz complied,

Heeding the advice, to the khan she'd ride.

Six companions by her side, she trod the way,

Before the ruler's presence, fearless, she'd sway.

With a gaze of anger, Khan Mambet stared,

But Narqyz's resolve remained unimpaired.

Unfazed by his fury, she spoke her mind,

Words of strength and truth, unconfined:

- You are the main protector of the people,

The overseer of this land so ample.

They call me the poet Narqyz, renowned in name,

My fame has spread far and wide, like flame.

Once named Aisha in days of old,

But my prowess and strength took hold.

Now I'm known as Narqyz, fierce and bold.

Summoned here by your decree,

I stand before you, ready and free.

For what purpose, pray tell me,

Have you called, or what may it be?

Do you seek a warrior's might,

Or is there another reason in sight?

My khan, please speak and be clear,

Is there a match for me to adhere?

My father, Seit, lacks cattle and sheep,

In poverty's grip, he struggles deep.

Not just food, but clothes he lacks,

A needy servant on poverty's tracks.

Your bald, bereaved brother

Knew of this from afar,

His people offered bribes

To my father, a meager star.

Sticky in his pursuit, he aimed for me,

My poor father couldn't decline, you see,

As the khan's elder brother, he held sway,

Submitting to the wishes, he had no say.

Advised by others, they whispered in his ear,

"A khan's lineage is needed," they made clear.

And he believed them out of fear,

Though woman by birth, my strength defies,

As strong as any man, my spirit flies…

Though rich he may be, not worthy is he,

Bald and flawed is not one for me.

Who's worthy of me, the choice is yours to see,

The right to decide, of course, lies within thee.

The Lion, your brother, did you see

With your own eyes, recently?

For your graciousness, my khan so kind,

You've honored me with favor undefined.

But can you truly hold the view,

Your brother's equal in strength to me, too?

If fairness guides your judgment's sway,

And grant me my freedom today.

Remember this wisdom of old lore,

"The khan's words is his alone,

But it carries forty advisors' tone."

Reflect upon it deeply, I implore.

We too, are your children, seek what's just,

If the khan fails to act with trust,

For whom shall our strength and valor accrue?

We're weary, seeking relief anew.

And our foundation is askew.

Since your summons reached my ear,

Here I stand before you, clear.

All power is yours, your grace supreme,

Grant me freedom to choose my own dream.

But the Khan ignored her plea,

Her words he chose to disagree.

The khan's comfort and peace, you see

She has troubled quite enough already.

The khan reached, but just out of grasp,

Desiring to seize the girl, alas…

Narqyz swiftly left the house's hold,

To her horse, she quickly strolled.

A friend of hers brought the horse,

Holding the reins with careful force.

She swiftly mounted, took her seat,

On the white horse, she felt complete.

She galloped off to her people's seat.

The wicked Mambet, dark as night,

Commanded soldiers, ready to ignite,

"Seize her!" he bellowed, his voice like thunder,

His guards set off, a chase to plunder.

The white horse beneath Narqyz's grace,

Sensed the pursuit, quickening its pace,

Ears pricked forward, it started to race.

The girl sensed the guards closing in,

Their shouts behind, a deafening din.

Narqyz tightened her grip with her calves,

Whipped her horse to clear the paths,

Uphill she rode with all her might,

The horse's sweat glistening in the light.

Foam flew from the bit from their flight…

The guards beheld the horse's speed,

Realizing the chase was doomed to recede.

They halted, heads shaking in defeat,

"We can't catch her," their words replete.

To all those gathered at this site,

Khan Mambet's order took its flight:

Bring everyone to me,- he decreed,

I have words to share, - his intent indeed.

They must grasp my thoughts profound,

And heed the words about to resound.

Narqyz has fled from my command,

They must seize her, bring her to this land.

At Khan's command, the people gathered 'round,

Hastening to heed the summoning sound.

The Khan sat fuming, swinging in ire,

His mood ablaze like a burning fire.

This is the decree for one and all:

Narqyz's insult upon me did fall,

My words she disregarded, my authority spurned,

Such audacious defiance I've not previously discerned.

Seize Narqyz at once, heed my command,

For this affront, she shall not withstand!

That is all I have to say to thee,

You shall heed my decree!

If my words are mere wind to you,

How am I the khan? Now, pursue!

Obedient, as oppressed slaves, they stand:

Your order's weight, a firm command.

From you it comes, we can't deny,

Accepting gladly, we comply.

Narqyz, who fled our sight today,

We'll seek her out without delay.

If she's discovered, we'll pursue,

And deliver her as you wish, true.

Boktergi, a troublemaker bold,

Mischievous deeds in his path he strolled.

To peaceful folks, he brought dismay,

Unjustly harassed, led them astray.

Slandering lives, causing strife and pains,

Inflicting trouble in his wicked ways.

To Mambet Khan, he came near,

Whispered slyly, fueled by his own fear:

"I'll catch that Narqyz girl for you, my lord,

I'll do what's needed, you have my word."

This word of Boktergi's

Mambet did gladly accept.

"Good, Boktergi, Boktergi!" he praised loyalty kept.

Brave men aplenty I've seen before,

But you're a man to admire more,

And so, you I admire, - he swore.

Bring the runaway Narqyz to me,

Into my grasp, from where she's free.

My anger's fire burns fierce and bright,

I'll cage her within my vengeful might.

When Narqyz you do bring,

I'll rend her to pieces with my fury's sting.

And you shall earn a friend's embrace,

Among the people, a favored place.

Boktergi combed through lands so wide,

Searching every corner, none could hide.

Counting heads, tallying each abode,

Seeking Narqyz on every road.

In a village with houses plenty,

One yurt stood out, its presence sentry.

To this nest Boktergi did head,

Approaching carefully,

Caution in his tread.

With her guards in tow,

Inside the white yurt

He found Narqyz, the girl of renown.

- Though famed you are, my dear

Young still you are, that much is clear.

You are brave, I understand,

At that gathering of tribes

I have seen your prowess grand.

You defied the khan's command,

Took a stance against his hand.

May your intentions pure remain, he spoke.

I am Boktergi, your uncle so dear,

Honey, be my guest without fear.

To guide you, dear child, is my aim,

An honor to help, I proclaim.

Come, let me lead you to my abode,

Where you'll find safety on this road.

Trust me to offer you aid, true and tried,

To be of service, with you by my side…

Well-meaning and sincere, she trusts

Narqyz believes in him, no doubts.

With Boktergi, she walks along,

To his home, they both head on.

With respect, he woos her in grace,

Gives a lavish guest dinner, a warm embrace.

The service he gives is in her taste:

- A good uncle, Boktergi, you've proven to be,

With care and kindness, you've set me free.

Your songs and entertainment are a joyful delight,

In this place of honor, you've made me feel right.

I am your sister and you are a brother,

Find someone worthy, like no other.

The khan's sibling, I cannot adore,

Born of privilege, yet I implore,

I won't love him, my heart is clear,

For he is not an equal, I won't touch smear.

Because I am Narqyz, you see,

Happiness is what I truly plea.

More than riches, it's joy that I chase,

To live with an equal, face to face,

Laughing and playing day by day,

That's the life I yearn to sway.

Without living with an equal near,

What's the happiness we hold dear?

Playing dombra, poems reciting,

These joys in life are quite inviting.

But dear brother Boktergi, hear me plea,

I grant you power to choose for me,

Find an equal, true and just,

I'll heed your words, do what I must.

You care for me, good brother,

To say more of you I wouldn't bother.

I can't trust anyone for this to do,

In you, my trust finds its avenue!

- My dear Narqyz, sweet as honey,

Feelings are right, they're never phony.

Now, you rest assured, please, you must

For we as a people have discussed,

As a collective, we deliberated,

An agreement with the khan is formulated –

Now, honey, your path is free and clear,

You can choose from anywhere far and near,

Find a partner, a love sincere,

Your choice is yours, my dear.

Someone worthy, whom you find dear,

You can go to without fear!

- Uncle, I believe you!

Thank you, dear uncle,

For your words that bring me joy.

You're a strong pillar, uncle dear,

When my spirits seem to toy.

With news that uplifted her spirits so,

Narqyz could finally let herself go.

Then ten young men approached with glee --

All from Boktergin's company, you see.

To catch Narqyz in their custody,

They watched the house carefully.

Boktergi goes a separate room of the house,

As if to skins a yeanling, quiet as a mouse.

With two long cotton belts, he weaves his plan,

A secret rope formed with a skilled hand.

Setting it down, his scheme began.

Unaware of the trap, Narqyz dines,

Filling her stomach with savory signs.

Brave and tired, she soon falls asleep,

Into a slumber, so calm and deep.

To check her sleeping, Boktergi sneaks around,

His intentions devious, his heart unbound.

He sees her deep slumber, so tranquil and pure,

Narqyz, a moon's radiance, of that he's sure.

But little does she know, danger lies in wait,

A trap set by Boktergi, sealing her fate.

As she peacefully sleeps, unaware of the snare,

He dreams of capturing her, his wicked affair.

Boktergi whispered to the outside ten,

"Narqyz sleeps now," he said to his men.

"Be careful now," he cautioned them.

The ten moved quietly, their mission spurred.

Into the house they crept, like shadows in the night,

To steal and seize Narqyz, hidden from sight.

Narqyz they captured, her fate to descend.

With no one to help and no way to defend.

Bound by ropes, Narqyz in despair,

Struggled and writhed, her spirit aware.

Hands and feet tied, a captive's plight,

She fought to break free with all her might.

With every ounce of strength she possessed,

She strived for freedom, her will undistressed.

Boktergi, her nemesis sly,

Bound her legs, oh my, oh my.

Gripping them with all of his zest.

She drew her legs close to her chest,

Kicking fiercely, she gave her best.

Boktergi reeled, his mouth did bleed.

The men who stood with him, confused,

Held the warrior's head, feeling used.

They were at a loss, unsure what to do,

Staring in shock, as if in a stew.

They brought trouble on themselves, alas,

Ran off and shared their tale with the mass.

After a couple of hours of craze,

Boktergi awoke from his daze.

A crowd had gathered in a throng,

Boktergi lay, weakened, his spirit not strong.

He saw the people around, aghast,

Gathering his thoughts, his life he recast.

He believed his end was nearing fast.

- You, people who have gathered here,

To our esteemed Khan and all, I hold dear,

In service, I have always stood,

But now I am shocked, misunderstood.

This pain I've caused is mine to bear,

My end is near, I feel despair.

Farewell to you all, I confess,

I won't live on, my life's a mess.

Forgiveness I seek in my final breath,

I acted for the Khan, in life and death.

If death should claim me now,

Tell Mambet Khan, my friend, somehow,

Let my honor be mourned and known,

In my absence, let my story be shown.

Mambet, my pal, should avenge my plight,

Pass my greetings to him, my last fight.

To the Khan, many greetings extend,

Let my departure not be a silent end.

We're not true humans, I say with clarity,

If our voices are silenced in obscurity.

Deliver my warm greetings to the Khan,

May my actions find favor in his plan…

With only one life and no way to survive,

No throat to quench thirst, no hope to revive.

He was lying on his back,

Helpless and almost still,

Life slipping away, an unyielding chill.

People gather around, witnessing his plight,

Boktergi's fate fading, the end in sight.

As the crowd that gathered swelled,

He kept on bidding his farewell,

In the evening's embrace,

His strength did quell.

Losing consciousness again and again,

Thoughts fading away at the end,

Goodbyes on his lips as night turned to gray.

Shaking everyone's hands, he said his last adieu,

Women and children wailed, grief in their view.

As darkness fell upon the land,

Relatives mourned, a sorrowful band.

"He leaves so young," they sadly sighed,

Misfortune's hand in his fate implied.

Twilight settled, stars adorned the night,

A time for farewells, a solemn rite.

In his final moments, he clung to the khan,

Dignity wavered, like shifting sand.

His every word echoed Mambet's name,

Yet subservience couldn't his fate reclaim.

He fought for honor, but soon life did wane,

From Narqyz's kick, his end came, his pain.

Bound at hands and feet, she was secured,

Tightly tied, her freedom obscured.

On a camel's back, they placed her with care,

To the evil Mambet's dwelling, they did bear.

And then Mambet speaks, his intentions clear,

His thoughts, he begins to share:

- You've taken a life, - he coldly declares,

Why did you do it? Speak, girl, I demand,

Give me your reasons, make me understand!

But she didn't agree to answer,

Pride strong, she held her stance,

The khan's fury, his face a reddened hue,

Fearlessly met, with unyielding advance.

She didn't respond to the khan's demand,

Refusing to utter a word in reply.

He persisted, his frustration evident,

"Give me an answer!" he continued to cry.

He stopped with the anger.

She still gave him no reply.

Just stood there unmoving,

No matter how hard he tried.

With rage coursing through his veins,

The black-hearted Mambet

Called on his men to come forth.

"Select your weapons," he thundered in disdain,

Bind her again to the camel's back, of her worth

Leave no trace of defiance, no stain,

Do whatever it takes, let her feel the full force.

The men, without hesitation, assembled 'round,

Effortlessly hoisted her onto the camel's back.

Bound her so tight, her struggles were bound,

They were relentless, no mercy did they lack.

Bound and helpless, Narqyz confined,

In this dire strait, her freedom declined.

Tied and trapped, her spirit declined,

In this somber hour, her strength reassigned.

In a solitary house, its door tightly sealed,

Narqyz was held, her fate now revealed.

Locked away in darkness, her spirit concealed.

Anger consumed her, sleep kept at bay,

Locked in that house, with no light of day.

Ten guards outside, vigilant, they stay,

Doors tightly shut, she felt like prey.

Bound tight with thick ropes, she couldn't break free,

Under immense pressure, still strong was she.

Narqyz, so beautiful, held her stance with grace,

Her anger, a tempest, in that confined space.

Despite the meals offered, she stood by her creed,

The khan's sustenance, she vowed not to eat.

No morsel or sip would pass through her lip,

In her unwavering spirit, she'd never slip.

Her heart burned with vengeance bright,

"I'll avenge myself on the khan!"
She vowed with her might.

Narqyz stirred a ceaseless storm,

In Khan Mambet's mind, her form.

And Narqyz too, with anger burning bright,

Thought of her honor, both day and night.

She was angry every night

And whenever she would scream

Khan Mambet who was sleeping

Would wake up from his dreams.

Narqyz, noble, mightier than Khan,

Stronger, smarter, with courage to stand,

Hungry and thirsty, she was bound to the land,

She shouted, trapped by his ruthless hand.

The Khan's many wives,

From brave Narqyz's screams so grand,

Lost their minds, by turmoil unmanned.

In fear of the girl, the women all around,

Whipped up their kumis, they pound.

Guilt-ridden hearts, with remorse they're bound,

They brought her food, feeling deep shame,

Narqyz accepted, playing no blameless game.

There was no one to help

No one she could count on

She was her own strength and power.

Such was the state of her

The one who was enemy of the khan.

Narqyz wished a wish, her heart's stern,

Tired of anger, her soul did yearn.

Hysterically, she laughed and would discern,

Moments of crying, emotions churn.

No permission for anything during her stay,

No glimpse of the sun's warming ray,

Hope in the Khan had faded away.

From the sworn enemy, no kindness at play,

In the depths of anger and disgrace,

Narqyz pondered her woeful case.

A daring thought began to trace

A fantasy in that darkened space:

Let me craft a clever scheme,

Not idly languish in this dream.

A stratagem, a secret gleam,

In the shadows, like a beam.

Regardless of my present plight,

I must gauge the khan's might.

Hear his words and in the night,

Curse him, for my future's bright.

Narqyz beckoned the head of the guards near,

To discuss matters the Khan should hear.

She sought an audience with the khan's grace,

To present her case face to face.

Invited, the head of guards drew near,

Asked Narqyz, her intent to hear,

"What shall you say?" he asked with a sneer.

Narqyz spoke with a voice firm,

You are the guard who watches term by term,

And I am your mere hostage in your realm.

Tell the Khan, this message affirm,

I've words for him, a concern to confirm.

Grant me leave to speak, please,

And I will let you have your peace.

Hurry to Mambet, don't be slow,

My words for him, you must bestow.

Mambet Khan, has taken me,

In anger and offense, you see,

He sits atop the ruling throne,

With crown, he reigns, his power known.

What I desire him to learn,

Is for a conversation, I yearn.

To have a dialogue, is it permissible?

Will Khan Mambet consider it sensible?

Or perhaps he'd come in person to see,

This ruler of the land, will he heed my plea?

Will he witness my tears, maybe?

Go relay this to the khan, let his response decree.

The guard heeded Narqyz's plea so clear,

He listened well, her words he'd hear,

Then to the Khan he did appear,

Reciting her message for him to steer.

Cruel Mambet, with a heart austere,

The message from Narqyz,

Has reached his ear.

The Khan found her plea agreeable,

Ordered her legs untied, an act commendable.

The ten guards, once stern and formidable,

Loosened the ropes of the hostage pitiable.

They brought her to the Khan by towline,

Upon his throne, resplendent and divine,

Khan Mambet awaited, his power did shine:

"Tell me your petition," he said.

- You've seen, Khan Mambet, the moves I've displayed.

Are your bald brother or the Lion, by any fair grade,

Truly my equals, or am I being betrayed?

Permit me the freedom, let no obstacle cascade,

Give me my freedom to choose, I implore,

For your brothers, born to the khan's noble lore,

Their status too high, this no one can ignore.

That is my plea, please, listen to me,

To the truth that I speak, I beseech,

You are on the throne,

You rule the people,

And are proud in your speech.

And remember that many

Have shown interest in me.

Your relatives are not my pairs, it's the truth I share,

If you should take me, take me yourself if you dare,

If you want, I will be yours,

For I know your worth, more than a trove

Mambet, it's you that I love.

You ponder, my Khan,

This thought I share,

Why choose the bald one, for I can't bear,

To be with him, it's not my affair,

I was disheartened

When you wished to make us a pair!

Please hear my words

You are at the center of the worlds

Righting the wrongs of the people

And you are our leader with no equals.

My khan wants to do justice

Even the blind can see.

Don't waste me please,

Make me a partner to thee!..

The khan grew pale,

Then his face turned red,

Torn between passion and thoughts in his head.

On one hand, the girl's fire he'd seen,

A woman for him, his heart did glean.

But doubts crept in, making his mind sway,

Narqyz, so sharp, wouldn't easily obey.

Her strength and her courage, he couldn't deny,

As his wife, she'd be fierce, not shy.

The khan, in turmoil, his feelings abound,

What a decision to make,

His thoughts spun round and round.

Interest won in the end, his heart did decide,

To take Narqyz as his consort, he'd confide.

You are worthy, Narqyz,- the khan did proclaim,

In my eyes, you shine with a worthy name.

Your beauty, like a jewel, fits a khan's grace,

You are an equal, in this sacred place.

I'll grant your wish, - Mambet's promise declared,

With Narqyz as his consort, he truly cared.

For if I don't take you, I wouldn't be content,

Without you by my side, my happiness is spent.

I won't shatter your peace,

Nor your joy I'll decrease.

In your happiness, I'll share,

Narqyz, you've found a pair so rare.

In this race of life, let me take part,

To win your lovely and gracious heart.

After we marry, you, Narqyz so fair,

Shall be the people's cherished, beyond compare.

What man wouldn't dream, in love so deep,

Of a consort like you, to forever keep?

In appreciation and love, our hearts will bind,

Narqyz, the beauty, to you, I'm inclined,

To make you the pride of all your kin,

Together in wedlock, our life shall begin.

Let me quench the fire, the flame inside you,

We'll move with haste, our love anew.

As I promised you, from this day hence,

You're free from bonds, no recompense.

I grant you, Narqyz, this heartfelt decree,

To choose your own mate, joyful and free.

No more shall you suffer, no more you'll pine,

Together we'll dance, our hearts entwined.

A yurt with forty ropes, a place so grand,

For all to see, in this blessed land.

With a sturdy iron door, strong and secure,

A haven of safety, that's for sure.

Ten guards, as before, yours to command,

By your side, forever, they'll stand.

Narqyz, her heart filled with secret delight,

Played her cards well, concealed her spite.

She smiled at Mambet, her act so convincing,

But vengeance within her, forever unrelenting.

She deceived the Khan with her clever disguise,

And thus, Narqyz triumphed in her guise.

Narqyz, with her deceit so sly,

Called him consort, oh, what a lie.

Mambet, the useless, had no clue,

Of Narqyz's plans, he never knew.

Short-sighted khans there used to be

Who would divide the people in the spree.

Such people ruled back then.

There was no freedom among men,

The khans could say whatever they wanted,

And their lies were usually taunted.

Yes, a time of chaos and whirlwinds,

Where strife and conflict constantly spins

People clashed, destroying life.

Strong dominated the meek,

In this world so wild and bleak.

Amidst the squabbling and debate,

Innocence met a cruel fate.

Blood spilled freely, hearts were chilled,

In this chaos, dreams were killed.

Niyaz from the Middle zhuz,

With fiery spirit, his cause he'd discuss.

"I seek those brave souls, willing to fight,

To challenge Mambet, to make things right," he cried.

His message spread, hearts were stirred,

Young men gathered, their voices heard.

On their steeds, they took their stand,

A growing force, across the land.

A hundred strong,

They stood with might,

Swords gleaming in the day's clear light.

With piercing spears and hearts ablaze,

Niyaz the warrior they chose to adore

Their fealty to him they all swore.

Their steeds were robust, their weapons shone,

Bows at their hips, a hundred as one.

Determined young men,

In their hearts the goal was set,

To overthrow Khan Mambet, to take his head.

Niyaz, though humble in his birth,

Radiated nobility, a man of worth.

In attire and steed, his stature clear,

A sturdy presence, no sign of fear.

Niyaz strummed the dombra, songs he'd bring,

Tales and tunes, he knew how to sing.

His lover, Akhyl, once stood by his side,

In her love and beauty, he took pride.

All who saw her were mesmerized and charmed,

By her grace and elegance, they were disarmed.

This was the reason he gathered the men -

There was a mission to be accomplished then.

Mambet had kidnapped his lover by force,

Akhyl the beautiful, with no remorse,

For that he was angry and got on his horse.

- Hey my hundred men, hundred men,

Stand by me, as my friends;.

To Mambet Khan's village,

I have decided to go;

For Akhyl, my bride, I'll strike a blow

Take her back and let him know;

The evil Mambet, black as night,

I will ride and I will fight;

Who will join me in in this test,

What say you to this brave quest?

The hundred men with vows sincere,

Mounted on horses, void of fear.

Bows were strung, and spears prepared,

As they rode forth, their mission declared.

Through hills and valleys, their steeds did prance,

Swords at their sides, ready for a dance.

With Niyaz as their fearless guide,

They journeyed forth, side by side.

They reached Mambet's village

In the middle of a shrouded night,

No moon, no stars, just darkness, no light.

They couldn't see a thing, the village obscured,

Yet Niyaz's determination remained undisturbed.

To capture Mambet, place his neck in a noose,

That was Niyaz's plan, he waited for cues.

Niyaz's anger simmered, a fiery tide,

Over to the horses, he strode with pride.

Where they grazed in pastures, he planned his way,

With his hundred friends, in ambush they'd stay.

They took their positions, a covert crew,

Causing commotion, their bold course they knew.

Startling the horses, with a thunderous clatter,

They drove them away, setting their strategy aflutter.

Niyaz's voice thundered, fierce and grand,

With a hundred warriors at his command.

"Where is Mambet the black?" he cried,

As they stormed the village, none to hide.

Khan Mambet, from his slumber, awoke,

In his voice, disbelief and shock spoke.

"What madness is this?" he cried aloud,

His question cutting through like thundercloud.

His first wife, with tears in her eyes, replied,

"It's sheer madness," she wept and cried.

The heroic brave Niyaz, with spear in hand,

Called out to the troublemaker, bold and grand.

"Come forth, Black Mambet, face your fate," he said,

Your worthless rule will now be shred.

Don't miss this chance, Khan Mambet, you see,

For vengeance is what I've come to decree.

I am Niyaz, your harassment won't stand,

Your reign of terror ends at my hand!

You've stolen my bride, caused me strife and dread,

I've come for revenge, Khan Mambet, you must know,

Your horses I've driven off, your house soon to be dead!

For the pain you've caused, for the love you've stowed.

In fear, he dressed in hurried strife,

Punishment has now come for him.

Around the house, he ran in strife,

Lost, confused, his vision dim.

Narqyz he thought was his safety's light,

In the dark, he dressed in fright,

His trembling bones in the still of night.

In his frantic plea, he implored for aid,

"Oh my God, Narqyz, don't let me fade!

My horde's in ruins, under attack so dire,

With spear in hand, he's setting us on fire.

The village is in chaos, a tumultuous stage,

Please, Narqyz, save me from this outrage!"

So pleaded Mambet, in fear and distress,

Narqyz, in her garments, prepared to address.

With pity in her heart, she had a plan,

To speak to Niyaz on behalf of the khan.

She came to him and said this:

- Niyaz the famed, your courage shines,

In this noble quest, your honor defines.

You've come to rescue Akhyl's grace,

Strong as a tiger in this dangerous place.

With poetic talents, your heart's like mine,

Artistic souls in this moment align.

You're fearless in battles, your fame extends,

Through the lands, your name transcends.

I've heard of your valor, none can deny,

No enemy dares your prowess to try.

You've come to challenge the khan's cruel reign,

Brave Niyaz, I won't call it profane.

To be frank, I feel a vengeance so strong,

I'll help you right this old grievous wrong.

If Mambet is the one you desire to take,

I'll give him to you, for revenge's sake!

With fearless might, Niyaz did steer,

His horse responding, victory near.

Narqyz, like an eagle bold in flight,

Swooped down and seized Mambet in her sight.

She held him like a prey in her grasp,

Brought him to Niyaz, just as fast.

Niyaz, the strongman,

Placed him across the saddle,

The khan's voice shrieked,

He began to prattle:

"Please, warrior, let me go,"

He pleaded his foe.

He loosened his hold,

Gave Mambet some room,

The khan was so shaken

In the dark, in the gloom.

As the brave Narqyz passed him over,

His fate was now unclear,

Then Niyaz inquired,

Her name he wished to hear:.

- When I look at you,

It seems I don't know you?

And when I hear you speak,

I know you're clever and bright,

Tell me your name, young fellow,

In this moonless night."

- Don't trouble me now

And I won't bother you, to that I'll vow,

Your request I'll respect, let's not delay,

No need for concern, I won't lead astray.

Return to your people, keep moving ahead,

Don't inquire my name, for now, it's unsaid.

We'll meet once again, in another display,

Perhaps then my name I'll willingly convey,

But for now, farewell, let's part and be free,

Our paths shall cross later, then you'll know me.

Take your trophy and be gone, my friend,

I'll come to you later, our paths will blend.

Mambet Khan on your saddle, you ride away,

But heed my words, and don't let them sway.

If you're true to your word, and strong of heart,

You'll wait for me after you depart.

We're equals, you and I, in this grand quest,

When our paths cross, we'll speak the rest.

You'll know who I am, of that I'm sure,

But if you're a coward, you'll flee, not endure.

Across many hills, you'll hastily roam,

Thinking this trophy's enough, to find a new home.

But if you wait, my friend, with courage and grace,

Another prize may await in this boundless chase.

The two warriors shook hands firm and true,

A silent pact made between the two.

With Mambet Khan placed across the saddle's span,

Niyaz rode off, a formidable man.

Having rid her life of this archenemy's plight,

The girl finally breathed, her heart feeling light.

Narqyz, in her heart so light,

Sang to herself through the night:

"O my land, so vast and grand,

Why should I not understand?

Your soul, once beaten,

Now stands free,

Your dark-hearted khan,

I can't foresee.

He's done his deeds, so vile and cruel,

Let him face justice, let it be his duel.

The brave can't be idle, it's true,

They must do what they're called to do.

For my nation, I'll stand tall and strong,

With a heart that knows right from wrong.

For my people, for their peace and grace,

I'll ride my white horse, set the pace.

With a sword at my side, a spear in my hand,

I'll avenge on Mambet, make him understand,

That justice will prevail, the truth we'll reveal,

I'll show him who's equal, with nerves of steel.

She called the stableman without delay,

"Bring my horse, my brave steed," she did say.

My noble steed, my faithful friend,

I've been a hostage, but that's at an end.

I've sent Niyaz off with a promise to keep,

The brave warrior, in whose hands Mambet wept.

Now I'll roam freely, among my kin so dear,

Reclaim our lost horses, make our enemies fear!"

The people who heard these words from Narqyz,

Were all in agreement, no need to quiz.

They brought her white horse with reins held taut,

She took her spear and on her horse she got.

Riding off boldly, in the sun's golden rays,

The people watched in awe, their voices a praise.

"She always keeps her promise," they said with glee,

A brave and true leader, for all to see.

With weapons chosen,

And a sword at her side,

Narqyz, the famous,

In her glory did ride.

Noble and strong,

Her beauty displayed,

On her white horse alone,

She journeyed unswayed.

She passed by the hills,

Now mountains ahead,

Whipped her white horse,

Over peaks she sped.

She went over one peak,

And then another,

Niyaz was true to his word.

He waited midway, as he said he would,

As Narqyz searched, as she said she would.

Singing songs, Narqyz passed her time,

Till the army appeared, in perfect rhyme.

She sped towards them, fearless and fast,

Reaching the front, the die was cast.

To the herd's leaders, she gave no care,

Just passed on through, in the mountain's glare.

Reaching the procession's very front,

Narqyz's journey continued, her spirit affront.

- I've come, Niyaz, as I said I would,

Delivered your enemy, as I should.

But I won't allow you to take away

The village's livestock, I must say.

Stealing is a dishonor upon our name,

Unless you return it, it's a cause for shame.

I came for the people's honor, my friend,

If you won't listen, then let's contend.

I challenge you now, let it be clear,

In single combat, unless you have fear.

Niyaz, on horseback, fierce and bold,

Charged straight at her, fearless and cold.

Their spears clashed with a mighty sound,

But neither could land a blow so profound.

Their tips shattered, hit the ground hard,

A duel of skill, neither caught off guard.

They fought with swords, fierce in their might,

On horseback in a tumultuous fight.

Punches thrown, hits they endured,

Their horses collided, strength ensured.

And in that fierce clash of horse and man,

The girl's helmet flew, not part of the plan.

Niyaz was shocked, his jaw agape,

The girl with braids had taken her shape.

Hidden scars beneath her hair,

A warrior, a girl, brave and rare.

"By the heavens!" Niyaz exclaimed in surprise,

"That I fought a maiden, none the wise."

He sheathed his sword, the battle ceased,

In awe of her courage, he called for peace.

- I can't bear another strike, it's true,

Though a man, defeat's what I've been through.

I've brought disgrace upon my name,

I heard tales of you, your warrior's fame.

Braver than most, they've often said,

Noble and strong, by many well-led.

The khan's brother, the mighty Lion,

You've left him limping, a laughable scion.

Now that I've met you, face to face,

Take back the horses, a sign of grace.

I've never seen a visage quite like yours,

Your expectations of a man truly soars.

Though I couldn't best you in this fight,

I accept defeat with all my might.

I yield to you, if that's your desire,

Make me your hostage, set my fate afire!

Narqyz gazed at Niyaz, taking her time,

In silence, she weighed his crime.

Choosing a punishment was not easy, you see,

But she decided, with little culpability:

- Your words, indeed, ring true and clear,

You've shown your character, you hold no fear.

I grant you forgiveness,

No ropes on your hands,

Your friends are free,

But obey my demands.

Take your trophy, the prize I bestow,

Now it's time for you to go.

- I have also enjoyed your speech.

You should also come with us, I beseech,

Meet my people before you go back.

I am a man, and have been beaten like a sack,

Bringing shame to my land.

- The people need Niyaz, a brave man,

Who will return the horses to their hands…

Niyaz was endeared, noble and exact,

Gave back the horses, no qualms or lack,

He'd give his head if she did ask,

Joined her journey, no longer a mask.

With two more men to help them guide,

The rest wished them well, no sense of pride,

"Have a good journey!" they all cried.

Narqyz brought back the mares and foals,

Ended Mambet's reign of controls.

"Cursed be his name, let evil retreat,

For better days ahead, a joyous feat.

With brave Niyaz, my lion, my might!,"

Narqyz hosted a feast, oh, what a sight!

Gathered her village, neighbors near,

Kumis for all, in a joyful cheer.

Placed her guests in seats of grace,

A grand celebration, in a merry place.

As Niyaz prepared to depart with the herd,

Narqyz shared her wisdom, every word heard:

- You are a cherished guest, my friend, so true,

Listen closely to what I now ask of you.

Summon Judge Bala of Middle Horde's fame,

And Judge Shonai, of the Lesser Horde's name.

Tell them to come swiftly, without delay,

Important matters we must discuss this day.

Heed my words spoken,

And be off on your way!..

The warrior Niyaz, heeding her decree,

Accepted her order willingly and free.

He dispatched a man to the Middle Horde's land,

To Judge Bala, an invitation so grand.

The messenger inquired, "What's this about?"

Understanding the stakes, no room for doubt,

Fair Lawgiver Bala, with twelve by his side,

Rode forth to the land where their summons did reside.

As Bala mounted his steed, word spread like fire,

Narqyz's yurt stood tall, her welcome entire.

With all due honors, she greeted the sage,

Her guest was esteemed in this golden age.

Bala and Shonai, lawmakers so fine,

With eloquent words like sweet, flowing wine,

Captivated the people, their wisdom they'd teach,

As guests of Narqyz, their presence did reach.

They lingered for days, in discourse they'd engage,

Satisfying their curiosity, turning the page.

After sharing their insights and what they knew,

Bala the judge gave a speech, honest and true.

In this time, not a typical speech you'll hear,

And Shonai is not a typical judge, it's clear.,

For the true lawmaker here, it's Narqyz's right,

She should have the final say, day or night.

Let her hold the power, the final say,

We'll accept her judgment, come what may.

In this way, we honor the people's voice,

Their wishes are our guide, the people's choice.

We won't create laws from above,

For the law should be born from the people's love.

Let Narqyz lead, with wisdom and grace,

And together, we'll find a rightful place.

Bala the judge began with eloquence and grace,

Shonai followed, keeping up the pace.

To conclude the speech, he made a plea,

Inviting Narqyz, for all to see.

Judge Bala and Judge Shonai, wise and true,

Made Narqyz the lawmaker, to justice she'd ensue.

The people agreed, their faith was strong,

In her wise judgments, they all did belong.

Narqyz rose up, her voice strong and clear,

To deliver her judgment, for all to hear:

- Striving for power and wealth, Mambet's reign did shake,

He stomped upon the people, their spirits left to break.

No longer shall he be khan, of my grand people's land,

Listen now to my judgment, I make this firm demand.

Judge Shonai and Judge Bala, heed my verdict true,

No longer shall he rule us, a better path we'll pursue.

Under the ruthless Mambet, we've borne a heavy life,

Now with fairness, compassion, we'll banish this strife.

Judge Bala, Judge Shonai, lead our nation strong,

Guide our people wisely, right any previous wrongs.

Protect the weak and hungry, shield them from the night,

Be the beacon of justice, our guiding, shining light.

The poor and the downtrodden, your care shall receive,

With fairness and compassion, their hearts you'll relieve.

With lawgivers Bala and Shonai, a future bright we'll share,

From now on, it's your duty to lead us with great care.

The judgement the girl Narqyz told

She gave purely from her heart of pure gold.

The gathered people, both young and old

Agreed to this judgment from Narqyz the bold.

From this moment on, their futures bright,

Two tribes could finally live in peace's gentle light.

Narqyz's words, in unity, they did heed,

Her wisdom shining, her people freed.

The people recognized the truth she spoke,

Accepted her verdict, harmony they'd invoke.

By the people's judgment, just and fair,

Nine camels to Niyaz, they did share,

Confiscated from Mambet, they did impart,

Happiness spread, filling every heart.

Niyaz spoke from his heart, sincere and true,

- Listen here, my friend, my dear,

Your beauty shines through.

You're my equal, my peer, and that's clear,

It's not trophies of another I pursue,

It's just you that I want, do you hear?

One of the judges, calm and not in haste,

Spoke kindly, with a gentle grace:

- Honey, I don't understand, you see,

When have I ever refused to decree

Happiness to a child's heart, carefree?

Niyaz loves you, it's plain as can be.

Don't be afraid, speak your heart's plea,

Let love blossom, let your love decree.

Narqyz, my girl, it's your destiny,

In this land where now your elders decree,

If you both agree, let love set you free.

- Everyone can find their soulmate, I suppose,

And to your wisdom, I respectfully pose.

If you both think Niyaz's love's the way,

I won't defy your words, come what may," she'd say.

"If you see in him a heart that's true,

I'll trust him too, as I ought to do."

Narqyz's reply was truly sincere,

Niyaz, her peer by age, brought her cheer.

As if Judges Shonai and Bala's wise hand

Paired a falcon and a swan on the land.

Once foes, now friends, their feud met its end,

Two peoples rejoiced, bonds they did mend.

Sheep were donated for the grand celebration,

A magnificent wedding, a joyful sensation.

Who could remain untouched, unswayed,

By such an occasion, the memories made?

The Middle Horde and Lesser Horde's hate did cease,

Niyaz and Narqyz, the harbingers of peace.

They mingled together like kith and kin,

No more enemies, but friends akin.

Of this people's life,

I could sing without end,

But for now, my dear friend,

Let this poem suspend.

The poem 'Narkyz' was published at the behest of the cultural fund named after N. Baiganin, the 'People's Akyn of Kazakhstan', with the support of the 'Kazakhstan Authors' Society' Republican public association.

Nurpeis Baiganin

About Author

Nurpeis Baiganin, a renowned Kazakh akyn, was born in the Aktobe region in 1860. Nurpeis developed a deep interest in playing the dombra and singing folk tunes at a young age. This interest was so strong in the young vocalist that he quickly earned the nicknames 'singer boy,' 'dombra boy,' and 'storyteller boy'.

Nurpeis, possessed an amazing memory, and eagerly listened to the best akyns of his time or their closest students, and memorized and sang their works by heart. His performing repertoire was filled at a young age with the songs and legends of the Western Kazakh akyns Abyl, Baitok, Sherniyaz, and Nurym, a fiery agitator and rebel leader Makhambet.

Nurpeis became a professional akyn at the age of 17. He competed and won in poetic competitions, known as aitys, with the famous akyns Kazakpay, Aktan, and Nuryn,. He made the tours customary for all akyns to auls (villages), and his name quickly spread not just in his homeland, but also in the Southern Urals, along the Syr Darya[1], in Karakalpakstan, Khiva, Turkmenistan, and elsewhere.

His extensive grasp of the Kazakh folk epic illuminated and sustained his performance. But Nurpeis did not simply rehash epic poetry; he recreated them, filled them with his vivid imagery, and performed them in his own dialect, making them closer, accessible, and understandable to ordinary people while still emotionally and symbolically saturated. In this manner, he createed versions of 'Orak and Mamai,' 'Qarasai and Qazi,' 'Er-Targyn,' 'Alpamys', and many more heroic poems. Nurpeis' works demonstrate a deep desire for honouring folk heroes, batyrs. The plot of the poem about the girl-batyr 'Narqyz' takes on a social element, with heroes combatting injustice and preserving not only their honour, but also the good of their country. Narqyz's fortitude stems

---

1   *Kazakhstan's main river, flowing into the Aral Sea*

from her intimate connection with her native land, family, and ancestors (Aruahs), and as a result, the people support her through hard times and motivate her heroism. The hero and the people's spiritual connection and mutual support will inevitably lead to victory.

In 1916, a new stream of inspiration entered Nurpeis Baiganin's work. Nurpeis developed as a fiery singer-agitator of the country's emerging trends. He sang about the leaders of the 1916 rebellion[2], Amangeldy[3] (Zhakip) and Karazhan, and his songs spread widely throughout the Kazakh steppes. The subjects and creative methods o his narrative songs expanded: taking the heroism of a distant, fairy-tale past, he incorporated them into the reality around him, not only in celebrated re-imaginings of folk epics to original works about both modern heroism and Kazakh everyday life. He wrote a poem called 'Akkenzhe' about the terrible fate of a young woman, telling the tragedy of a wasted young life in simple and plain language, with sympathetic images. The song is an indictment of the barbaric customs of the time, based on centuries-old traditions, of rampant bureaucratic arbitrariness and corruption, and of violations of basic human rights.

The events affecting his country's key events found expression in his work. The extraordinary exhilaration of feelings, the richness and variety of elaborate images and poetic vocabulary, the clarity of thought, covering the essential moments of Soviet reality - all othese qualities of Baiganin's post-revolutionary songs elevate them to unrival;ed examples of political lyrics of the time.

The language of Nurpeis Baiganin's writings is so metaphorical and light that his phrases became aphorisms, proverbs, and sayings in national discourse.

In recognition of the significant contribution of the people's akyn Nurpeis Baiganin to the country, the Soviet government bestowed upon him the title of Honoured Art Worker of the Kazakh SSR in 1939, and the Order of the Badge of Honor on him on his 80th birthday in 1940.

---

2   *The Central Asian and especially Kazakh rebellion against Tsar Nicholas*
3   *Amankeldi Imanov was one of the leaders of the 1916 Rebellion and became a Kazakh folk hero.*

A Review Of Nargyz: Unveiling the Poetic soul of Kazakh nomadism and linguistic resilience

The translation of the renowned Kazakh poem, Nargyz, into English marks a significant milestone in the cross-cultural exchange of literary treasures. This poem, deeply rooted in the nomadic traditions of Kazakhstan and the vast Central Asian Steppe where peoples have lived for tens of thousands of years, offers a unique window into the lives, values, and poetic expressions of a people whose existence has been intricately tied to the vivid landscape and the animals that inhabit them. It captures the legendary account of a courageous female warrior and leader called Nargyz whose spirit and passion communicate so much value for us today.

A special mention must be made, from the outset, to recognise the immense achievement this publication presents. It is an effort spanning multiple generations and begins with the highly renown national aqyn or improvisational poet, Nurpeis Baiganin (1860-1945) who would compose poetry as he was performing it. Nurpeis Baiganin composed this epic tale in his native Kazakh. It has been translated by the highly capable polyglot and narrative expert Elden Sarybay in what was clearly a magnificent labour of true love. The publication is beautifully illustrated by the talented Akmaral Zharaskyzy whose use of colour and form depict a dreamy world which is at once close to our imaginations yet far enough to be a majestic and unattainable domain.

Nargyz is originally in Kazakh which belongs to the Kipchak branch of the Turkic language family. This language has a rich and complex history, shaped by various historical events including the migrations of Turkic tribes, the Mongol invasions, and the establishment of the Kazakh Khanate in the 15th century. The Bodleian Library in Oxford has numerous artefacts which show the deep linguistic heritage of the Kazakh language and its ability to absorb and integrate words from other languages, particularly Persian and Arabic. The spread of Islam in Central Asia introduced Persian and Arabic influences, which have significantly enriched the Kazakh vocabulary. Many words related to religion, science, and administration have Persian or Arabic origins. For instance, words like world and school are borrowed from Arabic, while words such as flower and bread have Persian roots. There is also significant sharing of poetry as a form of communication and expression so whilst Persian and Arabic poetry features with some renown in the wider world it is now time for us to appreciate that Kazakh poetry is also of immense value.

Nargyz showcases a unique interplay between metre and motion, reflecting the nomadic lifestyle of the Kazakhs. The metre often mimics the gait of the animals that carry the nomads across the vast expanses of the steppes. For example, the poems rhythmic pattern can evoke the steady trot of a horse or the slower, more deliberate pace of a camel. This symbiotic relationship between metre and motion is not merely aesthetic; it is a reflection of the nomads' deep connection with their environment and the creatures that facilitate their movement. The translator has excelled in carrying much of the original tempo into the English version making it highly evocative as we accompany Nargyz on her numerous adventures. For example when travelling on horseback, the metre of Nargyz takes on a dynamic, almost galloping quality. The lines are often short and punctuated, mirroring the quick, rhythmic beats of a horse's hooves on the open steppe. This creates a sense of urgency and freedom, capturing the exhilaration of riding across the endless plains. In contrast, sections of the poem that describe travel by camel adopt a slower, more measured pace. The lines are longer, and the rhythm is more deliberate, reflecting the camel's steady gait and the nomads patient endurance. We must remember that poetry is not meant to be read but rather it is meant to be recited, to be declaimed, to be performed. For adults, teens and children there are so many wonderful excerpts which will effortlessly land in performances in family homes, schools and public arena.

Amongst the imaginings is the depiction of the terrain itself which plays a crucial role in shaping the imagery and tone of Nargyz. The Kazakh steppes, with their rolling hills, vast skies, and occasional oases, provide a backdrop that is both beautiful and unforgiving. The poem vividly describes the changing seasons, from the harsh winters with their biting winds to the lush summers filled with wildflowers. These descriptions are not mere embellishments; they are integral to the nomadic experience, where understanding and adapting to the environment is a matter of survival.

The imagery in Nargyz is rich and evocative, drawing heavily from the natural world. The poem speaks of animals, the environment, the weather and the human experience of the endless expanse of the steppe stretching out to the horizon. These images are not just poetic devices; they reflect the nomads' deep respect for nature and their place within it. The relationship between the nomads and their environment is one of mutual dependence, and this is beautifully captured in the poem's vivid descriptions.

Animals are central to the nomadic lifestyle depicted in Nargyz. Horses, camels, sheep, and goats are not just livestock; they are companions, providers, and symbols of wealth and status. The poem celebrates the strength and beauty of these animals, often personifying them in ways that highlight their importance to the nomads and even in the final movement of the poem it is through animals we see evidence of how the various characters expressed their emotions and what value they placed on others.

Nargyz is a poem that transcends its cultural origins, speaking to universal themes of love, honour, and the human connection with nature. As we delve into its verses, we find ourselves transported to the vast steppes of Kazakhstan, experiencing the beauty and resilience of a nomadic lifestyle that continues to inspire and captivate us today. The poem, written largely in the present tense carries us along with the narrative and its use of metre, imagery, and linguistic adaptations makes it a powerful testament to the enduring spirit of the Kazakh people, their language and their admirable centuries' old culture.

— Ar Amin

Narqyz: A Timeless Epic Bridging Kazakh Heritage and Modernity

The epic poem Narqyz by Nurpeis Baiganin, edited and translated for a contemporary audience, is a profound preservation of Kazakh oral tradition and storytelling. This 2024 publication by Hertfordshire Press introduces English-speaking readers to the rich tapestry of Kazakh culture through the lens of one of its most celebrated aqyns (poet-improvisers).

The work stands out as a literary artifact, capturing the oral heritage of a nomadic people where storytelling was both a communal and a personal art form. Baiganin's Narqyz goes beyond mere historical preservation; it is a vivid narrative that reflects the societal values, struggles, and triumphs of Kazakh life. The titular character, Narqyz, is a bold and multifaceted heroine—a wrestler, poet, and fierce advocate for her autonomy. Her journey not only embodies the valor traditionally celebrated in Kazakh epics but also challenges patriarchal norms by centering a woman's strength and intellect.

Interestingly, Narqyz's character resonates with the personality of Banucicak from the ancient and renowned Dede Gorgud epos, a cornerstone of Turkic oral literature. Like Banucicak, Narqyz exemplifies courage, wit, and unwavering determination, challenging the societal expectations of women while serving as a unifying force in her community. Both figures symbolize the blend of warrior strength and poetic intellect, embodying the ideals of resilience and leadership in their respective narratives.

The poetic style is intricate and rhythmic, echoing the improvisational flair of aqyns. Baiganin's ability to reimagine ancient tales in a manner that resonates with modern sensibilities is a testament to his artistic prowess. This edition benefits greatly from the translation efforts of Elden Sarybay and the editorial vision of John Farndon, who ensure the poem retains its cultural authenticity while being accessible to an international audience.

The illustrations and design further enhance the reading experience, offering visual context to the rich narrative. Narqyz is not just a story; it is a cultural bridge, inviting readers to experience the enduring legacy of oral poetry and the spirit of the Kazakh steppe. This publication is a crucial addition to world literature, celebrating a tradition that connects past and present with eloquence and vitality.

— Zaur Hasanov, EGC Ambassador in Azerbaijan
and the winner of OCABF 2014